Get Rich with Rentals

By Katherine Flansburg

Table of Contents

Introduction

Back in 2004 I decided I wanted to do whatever it took to get my foot in the door in real estate. I took home-based courses, classroom-based courses, read tons of books, and took real estate agents out to lunch in my town. However, none of that education gave me as much useful information as one week of onsite, real world real estate experience.

Thanks to people I have met and positions I have held, some days I feel like I have seen it all! I have had some interesting opportunities cross my path in the past few years. I have worked for a Fortune 500 new home builder, a distressed foreclosure warehouse, a mortgage bank, a busy small-town real estate brokerage, and as an independent real estate Broker myself. I have managed my own rental properties and I have helped dozens of investors choose and purchase their own rentals in dozens of states.

There are so many books out there telling you how to get rich quick in real estate. They all seem the same; they are all so vague. This book is a little different. Here you will read about real people who carefully started investing in properties. You will uncover some good tips for use in the real world. Some of my examples are incredibly specific. Maybe you can replicate them with good results, too.

You will also get a lot encouragement from me. As I write this in 2012 I keep thinking one thing: I hope Americans are beginning to see that this is the perfect storm; now is the time to begin seriously searching for solid investment property.

Chapter 1

What If?

In the summer of 2006 I met Lily, a nurse who noticed a little blue house for sale 3 doors down from her mother's place. Lily was 40 and had never purchased a house before. She lived well within her means and owned a 20-year-old mobile home.

We arranged to meet at the little blue house and her mother walked over from her own house, identical in every way except that hers was white. All the houses on this particular street were built in the 1950s. Back then, the builders had decided on a single floor plan; a 3 bedroom, 2 bathroom home with a tiny attic and a single-car garage. Even though 5 decades had passed, the house was still a pleasant and open floor plan.

In 2006 the little blue house Lily liked was listed for $250,000. Where Lily was shopping in Lancaster, a town in northern Los Angeles County, this was a pretty attractive price. Most single-family homes were listed over $300,000 at that time. As we walked through the simple home Lily inspected every detail and measured all the rooms. Her mother teased Lily about buying a house exactly like the one in which she grew up. I asked the mother how long she had lived on that street.

"Oh," she said. "My husband I bought ours brand new from the builder in 1957. We paid $5,000 for it. Now I wish we'd bought a few more."

Lily's mother never owned a rental home. She and her husband simply bought a home for themselves and raised a family in it. Without taking into account inflation, Lily's mother held an asset worth 50 times what she paid for it. After I dug a little deeper into her story, I found out she had not made a house payment since 1972 when they paid off their mortgage early. Her husband passed away in 2001 and she did not need to move to a more affordable place. Because she owned her home, she could stay exactly where she wanted to be. Their investment was sound and successful from every angle. But, like Lily's mother said, what if they had bought a few more?

Chapter 2

Before You Shop

What do you want your rentals to do? It is important to decide exactly what you want your rental to do for you before you start shopping. I say *before* you shop because once you start looking at homes, emotions take over. Salespeople know that buyers purchase homes based on emotion, then later justify the purchase to themselves logically. As a new investor you have to make certain you are consciously acting with logic first.

You may buy a home that you really like, but that does not mean it is going to perform in the way you expect it to if you do not shop strategically.

Rentals can accomplish lots of different things for people.

Rentals can:

-Hold equity for use in future uncertain times

-Generate passive income

-Be a hedge against inflation

-House your college-aged child for the 3 to 10 years he/she attends a university

-Become a personal empire

-Be a planned inheritance for your children or spouse

In the next few chapters we will expand on these so you can gain a clear idea of what each example really means.

Chapter 3

Elusive Equity

Holding equity: This means owing less money on a property than it is worth. If the home is worth $80,000 but you owe $30,000, then you have $50,000 in equity.

It is never easy to find a home for sale that is accidentally priced too low. Some investors work all day, every day looking for homes they can buy for significantly less than they are worth. If you intend to make real estate investing a full time job, this might work well for you. Deals are always out there, you just have to keep looking until you find them.

Full-time investors go after low-priced deals a few different ways. They seek out sellers who have been hit by one of the 3 D's. The three D's are Death, Divorce, and Debt. People who have been affected by one of these three tragic events are motivated to sell quickly. The main idea is that investors buying in these situations have the position of strength; therefore they can negotiate significantly lower prices.

During the past few years the three D's have not been hunted as relentlessly as they once were. With the flood of foreclosures a new cat came to town: the REO. REO means Real Estate Owned. Real Estate Owned by the bank, that is. The banks did not want these upside-down houses back, but hundreds of lenders foreclosed when owners stop paying the monthly mortgage payments. Real estate investors across the U.S. have recently been buying up REO properties for bottom dollar. Some have been working and buying through the Realtors listing these REO properties. Others have been working to buy multiples directly from the banks themselves. In short, any way a real estate investor can find to buy a home for less than it is worth is a way to maximize the equity position.

Another way to gain equity is to find a home with a problem you can fix to generate equity soon after you buy it. This is, simply put, when you look for the worst house on the best street. Maybe the house desperately needs an updated kitchen and the fluorescent lighting removed. If you can buy the home for $15,000 under market value and renovate the kitchen for $5,000, then you can generate $10,000 in equity you didn't have before.

As you look for your first properties, I suggest you buy your first investment close to home. Why? Because this is an area you know. You know the schools, the neighborhoods people think of as the desirable ones, and the commuting distances to the major employers. And if you realize you do not know your town particularly well, reach out to a real estate agent to help you.

Careful, though. The first month I worked as a real estate agent I sat in a cubicle near my broker, Mike. He was an incredibly busy, successful real estate broker and he met with buyers and sellers in his office all day long. Mike's office had a large glass window and door, so I noticed when his clients were acting unusual.

One afternoon a tall young man jumped out of his seat across from Mike, wrenched the door open, and stormed through the office. Once the man reached the parking lot, I turned back to sneak a look at Mike. He had an amused expression on his face.

"What happened there?" I asked.

Mike chuckled. "He told me he only wanted to see houses that he could do less than $5,000 of work on and then sell for a 20% profit within 6 months. I told him I could show him a few places if he wanted, but he should be aware that if I came across any properties like that I would probably buy them for myself."

I was so new in the business it had never occurred to me that I might find a property with such huge potential that I would want to jump on it before one of my clients did. In fairness, Mike was not trying to go out of his way to be rude or unethical; he was trying to make the buyer understand that these kinds of deals were not easy to find.

Beware of this scenario when you start looking. If you ask a pro for help, sometimes he might just help himself. Sometimes you have to hunt down the best deals for yourself!

Chapter 4

Passive Income

Generating passive income simply means earning money without exchanging time for money. In other words, you don't have to show up to a 9 to 5 job in order to get a paycheck. The idea is that the paycheck comes whether you do anything or not.

I strongly believe the term "passive income" gives the wrong impression. Rentals need work and attention. Tenants need landlords who communicate quickly and fix maintenance problems right. Landlords need tenants who pay in full and pay on time. Property inspections need to be performed so mold and leaks are discovered early. Accounting needs to be up-to-date so rental deposits are not illegally funneled to surprise tax bills or, even worse, negative monthly cash flow.

This is one area where I strongly recommend enlisting a real estate agent or property management team to help you. In California I knew a husband & wife team who were simply born to manage rentals.

Carl and Betty worked out quarterly calendars and visited around 30 properties each month on a regular, rotating schedule. Each lease they managed included a clause stating that they would enter the property every 3 months to inspect and take pictures for the property file. During these visits, Carl and Betty discovered issues the tenants, for whatever reason, kept silent about. They found things like a covered patio separating from the house structure, a leaking pipe in a laundry room that had set off a nasty mold growth, fire damage in a kitchen from a grease fire, and destructive pets unlisted on the rental agreement.

Carl and Betty notified the owner/landlords early enough to keep problems from spiraling out of control. More importantly, they handled the problems. They handled the evictions and the midnight emergency phone calls. In 2008 they charged 10% of rents collected. If the tenant did not pay, then the managers did not earn anything. These 2 property managers were careful about screening tenants. Naturally they wanted to receive their money every month, too.

It took Carl and Beverly 20 years to build a property management business of that size. By that time they were established well enough to turn down the management of rentals that did not meet their high standards of condition, too. Let's do the math on their gross earnings.

We'll assume: average rent collected at $1,500 per house. Average percent of tenants who paid each month: 95%. Carl & Betty were usually managing 100 houses every month.

So 10% x 1500 x 95% x 100 = $14,250

And they were worth every single penny.

I know about most of this because Carl and Betty took time to teach new real estate agents in continuing education courses. They made a good living, even after all of their mail, gasoline, and office expenses, just by running their property management business. They made a great living, however, by owning and renting 20 of their own properties purchased over 20 years in the business.

Let's do the math on their gross rental earnings. Average rent collected at $1,500 per house. Average property tax and repairs estimate at 10% of gross rent. Assume an average occupancy rate at a high 90% since they are tenant selection pros. Also, Carl and Betty held small mortgages and paid $5,000 in total each month to a credit union.

($1,500 - $150) x 90% x 20 = $24,300, then $24,300 - $5,000 = $19,300

Did I ever hear Carl or Betty refer to their income as passive? Not one single time.

Chapter 5

Hedging Your Bets

What does it mean to hedge against inflation? Since homes generally increase in value as time passes and inflation occurs as time passes, homes are considered a place to park money so that its value does not erode with time. Remember Lily's mom? If she and her husband put $5,000 in glass jars and buried them, it sure wouldn't be worth much today. But instead they invested it in a house, so it grew into $250,000 by 2006. It is a pretty simple idea, right? It just sounds intelligent and complicated, so people selling real estate love to mention it!

Holding real estate is a pretty reliable way to build wealth while at the same time hedging against inflation. One of the reasons is that the owner does not pay capital gains tax until the property is sold. Investors do pay tax on the money the house generates for them during the year, but the equity is not taxed until it is cashed out later.

Chapter 6

The Old College Try

Housing your college-aged student by investing in a rental property is one way to get started.

This is one rental purchase strategy that gets me really excited. Why? Because housing is one of the most expensive components of student costs while attending school. At the low end, a student at a university can rent a room for around $350 each month. If they study through the summer, then each year they are spending $4,200, and they are probably accomplishing this with a student loan. That might not sound like much in terms of housing costs or paying down a mortgage, but at the end of 3 years (the short end of finishing a Bachelor's Degree) they are dragging around $12,600 in loans they might have otherwise avoided. And this is only if the student has managed to refrain from signing up for an apartment or single dorm room. At notoriously affordable universities like Texas A&M, graduate housing with a single bedroom costs over $700 a month.

And what if your rising star continues through 6 years of college? We are talking about some serious money now. It is growing to be the equivalent of a down payment on a nice house, or a year of tuition at a top notch school.

There are hundreds, if not thousands of investors in the U.S. who stick exclusively to college towns. Why? Because there are thousands and thousands of students moving into the area every year with no intention of buying a place to live. They need to live near the campus and they have money to spend. The cleanest properties closest to the campus often command 2 to 4 year leases, as well.

So let us pretend I have a responsible 18-year-old I am planning to drop off at college in August.

Right now I am looking at my Trulia iPad app (yes, it's free) and I see at least 20 properties priced under $100,000 in College Station, TX. You can also just check out www.trulia.com. The only information I am missing for number crunching is the HOA amount on a few condo properties. I like condos because they do not have yards. It makes it easier when there is no lawn for a tenant (or my hypothetical student) to forget to water.

I found a couple of properties worth exploring and I e-mailed a real estate agent in the area to ask her how much the HOA fees are. They average $150 a month. One property I am seriously interested in is a one bedroom unit on the ground floor. It is priced at a jaw-dropping $49,000. It has all the features a student will require, too. It is 1.5 miles from campus. There are washer & dryer hookups in the kitchen. This particular unit includes the washer & dryer with the sale, so that is a bonus. The stove, refrigerator, and countertops are all present and look clean. One thing I already know I will have to change: the filthy carpet I can see in the living room. I will never, ever own a rental with carpet in it. Carpet harbors smells, stains, and fleas. Choose a quality wood laminate or, primarily in hot states, a neutral tile.

So let's do the numbers on this investment for my college student. I am going to take out a traditional investment mortgage, so I need a 25% down payment. That is pretty typical for a conventional loan from a bank for an investment property. On $49,000 this means I need to invest $12,250. Let's assume I pay full price but the seller pays the closing costs and title fee. If my mortgage interest rate is 6%, then my monthly payment on a 30 year mortgage will be $220.33. The HOA is $150. Texas property taxes usually hover somewhere around 2.25% (it's calculated on the assessment of the property value and you should check with the county assessor before you buy) so it will be about $92 per month. To house my student will cost me $462.33 each month, plus utilities. Home Owner Associations often include water, so the utility in this case will only be electricity because the building does not have gas.

Now, this is a case of me being a kind investor-parent. There are a couple of other ways for me to handle this. If I spend $99,000, then I can secure a three bedroom condo and rent out 2 of the rooms while my student lives rent free. If I collect $350 from each of the other 2 students, they will pay my mortgage and my student's housing all the way through college with that $700 total each month.

Another thing I could do is allow my student to go ahead and take out the student loan for housing anyway. Then the student pays me the market rent, which in turn pays the mortgage on the condo. When the student graduates, we rent the condo to a new student and the profit pays the student loan payment until it is wiped out.

Here is an example of how this might work:

The student pays $500 per month for 4 years to live in the rental. This comes to $24,000 in student loan debt. The student moves out, and now the market rent is $650 for this property. If we put $38 each month toward future repairs in a separate account, then there is $150 profit we can direct toward the student loan payment.

In the future, I have the option of selling the condo so I can recoup the cash I originally invested. Then I could gift my child any overage toward paying off that student loan. Alternatively, we could continue renting the property to students until it is paid off. Then my child could inherit an income-producing property. The possibilities truly are endless.

You are starting to understand how Fraternity and Sorority Houses come to be owned by their respective Fraternities/Sororities, aren't you? Put 10 students together times $350-$500 per room and these kids have $3,500-$5,000 towards expenses and a mortgage every month!

Chapter 7

Laying a Solid Foundation

Building a personal rental empire takes time and careful planning. Remember Carl and Betty? They acquired one home per year on average. That may seem slow, but for an individual investor that is a good pace that will keep debt under control. Can you imagine buying five homes in one year and then trying to service half a million dollars in debt while dealing with three vacancies? It would not take long for the average investor to throw in the towel. Move at a reasonable pace and move with purpose.

Carl and Betty had a distinct advantage over part-time investors. Every single day they were in neighborhoods, driving through areas they might never see if they held regular jobs. Their management work gave them a window few have the option to gaze through. They managed rentals all over town, so they knew a lot about every neighborhood. They knew what interior finishes, bedroom counts, and size of backyard commanded the highest rents. Since they helped landlords find contractors licensed to do plumbing and carpentry work, they developed relationships with skilled and fair professionals. Whenever Carl and Betty found a house to purchase as a rental, they called on the people they already trusted to prepare bids on jobs to get their new rental ready for the market.

Carl and Betty were careful with their cash in the early years. Carl worked the property management business alone in the beginning. Later, when there was enough property management work, Betty left her job as an insurance adjuster. Only when they paid off their own home did they start buying rentals for themselves.

Please avoid using your own home's equity to purchase rentals. I have worked with dozens of investors across several states. Investors who own their own home sleep better, think better, and earn better. Gambling your home is not a good way to start on your investment career. Live in a home you can truly afford and do not make any move that puts your own home in harm's way. There is no feeling better than owning your own home outright. Pay off your mortgage early, and do not refinance your home to get your hands on cash without careful deliberation.

Empires should be built on solid foundations. Your own home is the base of that foundation. If that means you live in a tiny, basic shoebox while you buy luxury rental properties, so be it. It still means a bank will not be able to take the place you call home because you found yourself in a situation where could not make the payments.

Chapter 8

Building Your Empire

The idea of owning dozens or hundreds of rental properties is intoxicating to investors. So how do the successful people really go about doing this?

In 2009 I discovered a Texas-based company with a unique business plan. I will call it NewVenture, but that is not the true company name. As an employee in the sales department I had a unique opportunity to see the good and bad side of how the process worked.

Shortly before the housing crash in 2008, three incredibly sharp men had an idea, pooled their money together, and started this small business with a few laptops and folding tables. All three had been buying real estate investments for decades. They recognized one of their biggest challenges was finding property priced low enough to yield a decent profit margin. If there could just be a single source it would make everything so much simpler.

These men also sensed the coming crash and realized that mortgage lenders would soon be offering large packages of homes for sale to the highest bidder. These 3 men were seasoned enough to remember when the banks sold packages of these distressed homes before. So that is exactly what they did. They set up this company to buy the property packages and then resell them individually for profit.

Here is an example of how this works. I do not want to pick on any lending institution, so I will simply call the seller Bank A. Bank A has 100 properties it foreclosed on the previous year. Bank A already listed most of these properties for sale with real estate brokers all over the United States, but for whatever reason the properties did not sell. Bank A puts all of these homes together into a package. Most of the homes are vacant and falling into disrepair. The values are only going down and the amounts owed on each for back taxes and HOA dues are only going up.

This package represents a major liability for Bank A and it needs to shift it quickly.

Bank A does not want these properties. Bank A wants money. So it lists the package for sale a few different ways. It uses its website, sends the information out to investor buyers who have purchased in the past, and may even offer it to another bank or investment trust. This package of 100 properties is not easy to sell for top dollar. There may be 45 states included in this list, and what single entity wants run-down houses in 45 different states? There are no pictures, no details like square footage or condition, and no guarantees. There may be renters in the houses, or the previous owners may still be living in a few. This package of 100 properties is a grab bag.

This is where NewVenture sees an opportunity. NewVenture finds out as much as it can about this list of properties through title records. They also look up expired listings online (the previous unsuccessful real estate agents created these) to find out more detail. NewVenture makes an offer on the entire package. The offer they make estimates at least a 100% profit margin. Anything less is too much of a gamble. In this grab bag of 100 properties, there are certain to be a few houses that are not worth even $1.

NewVenture is successful; it wins the bidding and buys the 100 properties for $800,000. This means they pay only $8,000 for each property. This is where it gets really interesting. NewVenture hires a few people to drive across the country to check on each house. They call these individual contractors 'assessors' since they are going to travel around assessing each property. Each assessor is assigned a region. One heads west to Arizona, New Mexico, and California. One heads to the northeast and visits Maine, New York, and New Hampshire. Another one visits 25 properties in Pennsylvania and wraps up with 2 in Illinois.

After each visit, the assessors e-mail information about the properties back to the main office. They also send digital pictures of the interiors and exteriors. As soon as NewVenture receives the information, the property information listing is added to the company website with photos. Before the assessors leave the properties, they put one sign in the window with the company name, web site, and phone number. Then they put another sign in the front yard.

Here is where the magic begins. Local people now know the property is for sale. Although these houses are not individually worth much to the investors at NewVenture, there are real opportunities for neighbors and local real estate investors. Phone calls start to trickle into the NewVenture office.

"Hello, I live next door to 123 Windsor Drive and I want to find out how much you want for it," says Buyer Brown.

NewVenture sales representative says, "OK, let me look it up. We just acquired that property from Bank A last week. After reviewing the assessment of the property we believe $25,000 is a fair price."

"No way will I pay that much," says Buyer Brown, "but I'll give you $18,000 for it if we can wrap it up this week."

"I can do $18,500 plus we charge $1,000 for transferring the deed to your name. If that works for you and you can sign our contract and wire us the funds by Thursday then we have a deal, Mr. Brown," says the sales rep.

"E-mail me the contract and I'll get started on it," says Buyer Brown.

What NewVenture did not know was that Buyer Brown made an offer to Bank A six months ago for the rundown house next door. At that time he offered $40,000, but Bank A would not accept it. What Buyer Brown did not know was that NewVenture only paid $8,000 for the place. Both NewVenture and Buyer Brown win big because Bank A is so overwhelmed with foreclosed houses that it cannot make careful, fully informed decisions as it liquidates each property.

There are several companies operating businesses like NewVenture now. They can be good sources for direct purchase, low-price real estate. They can also be sources of major headaches.

I mentioned that some properties would not be worth even $1. That can be hard for some people to even imagine. Every property should be worth at least a dollar, right? Many are *not*. For example, one home I sold for NewVenture had 4 feet of standing water in the basement. The home was in Minnesota and had not been winterized. Every pipe burst during the winter while the house sat vacant. Then, all the copper piping was stolen. Destroyed drywall covered the floors, caved ceilings hung bloated in midair, and warped wood ruined the curb appeal. The house was uninhabitable and structurally unsound.

The cost of demolition hovered somewhere around $10,000. Once that was complete, the final bill to the city for unpaid citations dating back 3 years totaled $5,000. On top of all that, there were unpaid property taxes. At the end of this exercise, the new owner would have an empty lot in a suburb worth between $7,000 to $10,000. The numbers did not make sense for anyone to be willing to pay even 1 cent for the property.

What happens in these cases? The city would eventually seize the property so they could get rid of the dangerous eyesore. If the city did not act due to lack of funds, in some cases neighbors would pool together to buy it and tear it down. They would do this especially if the property negatively affected property values surrounding it.

So who purchased the Minnesota property? The owner of the demolition company, of course!

Chapter 9

Sourcing Your Next Property

Another way to begin sourcing properties to start your real estate empire is through the U.S. Department of Housing and Urban Development. The website is www.hudhomestore.com. There, you can search low priced properties by individual state. HUD prefers to sell homes to people who plan to move in and occupy the home, but if there are no owner occupant bidders then they will consider offers from investors.

No matter where you find your real estate deals, one thing is certain. The place is going to need some work. I cannot say this enough. Always, ALWAYS get a home inspection. These days a licensed home inspector costs about $400. He or she will visit the property for a few hours and complete a written report. If the home is unusually large or dilapidated the inspection will cost significantly more.

I sold new homes for several years and was amazed by how many people skipped the home inspection. It is possible that the new home buyers skipped inspections so often because they reasoned since the home was new and under warranty everything should be ok. Well, what if the builder goes bankrupt? Many builders did between 2008 and today! It does not matter if the home is 2 hours old or 200 years old. For Your Protection -- Get a Home Inspection!

Once, I was working in a new home sales office and I received a call from a woman who had purchased a home from the company 4 years before. The builder had forgotten to put any insulation in her attic whatsoever. We were in the high desert in California! Her air conditioning bills had been, literally, through the roof! She had decided to have a contractor out to give her an estimate on increasing the insulation up in the attic because she didn't want to have another summer with $700 electric bills each month. When he came down the ladder and told her she did not have any insulation up there she could not believe it. It was unintentional and the builder did make everything right in the end, but a simple home inspection would have caught that oversight before she moved into the house.

Before you buy the home you are considering, get it inspected and then get bids on the work you believe needs to be completed. When you have the inspection and the bids you can negotiate price with the seller. Being 100% informed about the money you will need to spend on the house gives you a solid point to continue negotiations with the seller. The seller never likes to give up money, but once they know what the inspector has uncovered it is unlikely they will want to give up and try to find another buyer who will simply tell them about the same problems. It is better to lose the deal at this point versus go along with a purchase price that is too high. Walk away from the property if the numbers do not work for you. This is why you developed your rental business strategy before you started shopping. Logic is considered first. The emotional desire to have the property is a distant second.

Another way to acquire property under market value is by going to a real estate auction. These are most often advertised in newspapers. Expect to bring a sizeable cashier's check with you before you are allowed to enter. In California many auctions require a $5,000 cashier's check and a photo ID at check-in. If you successfully bid on a property, you can lose this deposit if you decide not to close on the home.

Real estate auctions are designed to shift tough-to-sell houses. You will come across homes with foundation problems and fire damage at auction. You may also see homes that are only half-finished because the builder went bankrupt in the middle of construction. Know your market, visit the property before you bid, and Get a Home Inspection!

Chapter 10

Short and Sweet Renovations

So what should you renovate? We will get to that shortly.

Here is the correct order for performing renovations.

1. Remove any flooring to be replaced
2. Ceiling repair and ceiling painting
3. Strip wallpaper, repair walls, paint walls
4. Paint and replace trim, including crown molding
5. Cabinet and countertop work
6. Install tile or quality wood laminate flooring (this may shorten the space for the appliances that go under the counter like dishwashers, so be careful with measurements pre-floor installation)
7. Install new appliances
8. Install base molding and baseboards in rooms with tile, vinyl, or quality wood laminate flooring
9. Install carpet (scratch that, NEVER put carpet in a rental)
10. Tidy up the landscaping

Renovations should be kept as simple as possible. It is important to make a house look its best before you rent it. It is in your best interest because updated, clean homes rent quickly and they rent for more money.

Since you are investing close to home to begin with, you probably have some idea of the features that are most sought after around you. Stucco exteriors are uncommon in Texas, and fireplaces are not required in Florida. Houses in Maine typically don't have air conditioners. Houses in Arizona probably need dual pane windows to keep cooling costs down. Know your area and do not add unnecessary features.

Flooring makes the biggest impact in a home. If the entire house is all one type of smooth flooring, then it looks much cleaner and larger. I think you already know my thoughts on carpet.

All the appliances in the kitchen must match! It is unacceptable to be anywhere outside of a low end college rental (maybe) and have a white refrigerator standing next to a black stove. While we are talking about stoves, keep this in mind. Women usually choose where the family is going to live. Her opinion carries great weight. In my experience selling hundreds of homes, women like to cook on gas. If you can possibly have a gas stove in the kitchen, go ahead and do it!

As you prepare your rental home to go on the market, aim to make this home look as clean as possible. Clean conveys many positive ideas: Caring, Upscale, and Convenient among them. People love clean cars and clean homes. To make a home look super clean, paint all of the walls a light neutral color and paint the trim bright white. You will need a durable, washable paint without a lot of shine. Keep it all one color and touch ups will be a breeze in the future.

Door hardware should be updated and functional. Caulk in the bathrooms and kitchen should be fresh and impeccable. If the countertops need attention, a Formica countertop with a granite pattern will be fine unless you are planning to operate in a luxury market. It is possible to install countertops for an entire kitchen in this material for under $500. This is very affordable and the tenants will be pleased that it is fresh and new for them.

Everything should work. There should be ice in the freezer, the doorbell should chime, and the garage door opener should raise the garage door. No part of the home should be storage for the landlord's personal belongings. If the thermostat is old, find out if the city will replace it for no charge. Programmable thermostats are now being freely offered by many cities to help keep electricity use under control in the summer. Find out if you can get a freebie.

Chapter 11

What is Section 8?

Lots of investors ask me about Section 8. Section 8 is formally called The Housing Choice Voucher Program. It is a federal program designed to assist families living in poverty as well as the disabled and elderly.

In the past few years it has become easier to advertise rental properties to the people served by the Housing Choice Vouch Program. The new website, www.GoSection8.com, allows landlords to enter information about their property and upload photos. In the past, landlords had to go to each Housing Authority and give all the details about the available property in person.

The part that attracts many landlords to participate in this program is the part where the Public Housing Agency pays a portion of the rent. The landlord has some peace of mind because he or she is not depending solely on the tenant for payment. Depending on the tenant's financial situation, the Public Housing Agency will pay a percentage (up to 100%) of the rent.

Things you need to know:

The house must be 100% safe. The wiring, flooring, door locks, lighting, cords on window blinds, stove, EVERYTHING will be examined. Once each year a housing inspector will make an appointment to come to the house and make sure everything is safe. If the house does not pass inspection, the authority will send a notice and you will not receive rent until the dwelling meets the requirements. The tenants may have to leave until the property can pass inspection.

This program is intended to help low income people secure decent, safe, sanitary, and affordable housing. The wait lists can be very long for tenants seeking assistance. Once they receive their vouchers places to call home, these residents are highly motivated to keep them.

I first learned about Section 8 housing back in 2005. It was a Saturday morning and Rueben and I were answering the phones at our real estate office in Lancaster. Both of us were real estate agents working under Broker Mike, and we were alternating the phone calls coming into the office that morning. Rueben had been working in real estate for about 5 years, and he was also a pastor.

The office was pretty quiet. We were drinking coffee, eating breakfast tacos, and reading the newspaper. There was an article in the newspaper about Section 8 that did not make much sense to me, so I asked Rueben if he knew anything about it.

"I rent to five Section 8 tenants right now," he told me. "It's a pretty good deal. You see, four my tenants are elderly. After I bought my first rental I heard about a lady named Cordelia. She was eligible for a Section 8 voucher but couldn't find anywhere to live that didn't have stairs. Well, my place didn't have stairs, so I gave her a call. After that I decided I would try to buy places with one or two bedrooms without any stairs. I was getting really good terms on the places I was buying because one bedroom houses and condos weren't really moving. And I didn't really need these places to have a garage because my tenants weren't driving, so I bought a few places really low and found people to rent them pretty fast. I did not even have to advertise after Cordelia moved in. Word got out and people started calling me and asking if I had anything available to rent. I make sure to put in a ramp if there are stairs at the front door and I keep all my rentals in really good condition. I had to put new walk-in showers with grab bars in 2 of them, but it was worth it. It took a while to get my first rent check that first time, but other than that I have only had minor problems."

Chapter 12

How to Work the Numbers

Let's talk numbers. Beginning investors need to know how much to offer when they find a promising property. This takes some knowledge and skill. Going out into the market and offering 50% on every property you see is going to get you labeled as a time waster. No one will take you seriously after a while. I read once that you should offer 85% of the list price. This sounds like a good strategy until you realize sellers very often list their homes for 125% of what they are worth. You can actually end up overpaying by doing this.

First, you need to know how much the property is actually worth. The best way to do this is to be an actual member of the Multiple Listing Service in your area. The only ways I know of to become a member include becoming a licensed real estate agent or becoming an assistant to a licensed real estate agent. Typical MLS dues are around $100 per month. If you do not want to become an MLS member, you need to start working with a real estate agent or a title person. Alternatively, you can camp out at the courthouse and review public records.

The only way to know what a property is worth is to know how much its neighboring homes are worth. Take a look at the websites at the end of this book to find some good property value resources. A home is only worth what someone is willing to spend to buy it. This sounds simple, but it is crucial. Many beginning investors overlook this.

You can ask the sellers how much they sold the home for if you can find them, but keep in mind that people are proud and often stretch the truth a bit. When you are a member of the MLS, you can log in online and see how much a home was originally listed for, how much it sold for, how many days it sat on the market waiting for a buyer, pictures of the condition, and the square footage of the property as reported by the seller, builder, or tax assessor. If you are working with a real estate agent, your agent can run a report listing all of this information for you. This report is called a CMA, or Comparative Market Analysis.

Once you actually know what the homes surrounding your subject property are worth, you can begin to boil down numbers. If your strategy is to generate monthly income, then you care most about the monthly rent revenue. Research how much money you can expect to collect every month. If the house is listed for sale for $120,000, needs no work, and the neighbors have sold comparable properties between $115,000 and $125,000 in less than 30 days, then you need to focus on the rental income because this is not a property for flipping.

Suppose you find that you can rent the home for $1,200 per month. If your combined expenses (mortgage, tax, repairs, HOA) are $900, are you happy with a $300 cash flow? If yes, start writing up a contract. You can still make an aggressive offer, just realize that in this situation the sellers are probably going to wait for a buyer willing to pay pretty close to market value.

A Focus on Flipping

Flipping has got to be the most adrenaline-pumping real estate topic in the U.S. Some television shows make it look easy, some make it look hard. My favorite part of some of these programs is the end. You know, the part when the purchase price, investment amount, and sales price are flashed up before the credits, but everyone conveniently forgets to mention the closing costs (often around $10,000). Simple closing costs can shrink a $14,000 profit down to $4,000 pretty quickly.

In the right situation, flipping can be a perfect exit strategy for a house. Here is an example of the right situation:

-you can buy the property for 75% of market value or less

-you are a tradesperson (plumber, electrician, or carpenter) and you can do a lot of expensive work at no cost

-you have reliable contractor contacts

-the market is actually moving and there are indications you will not be sitting and holding this house for 6 long months after it is finished

Some things I hear about that make me cringe:

-borrowing Hard Money with exorbitant interest rates to fund a Flip

-buyers planning to do all plumbing, electrical, and tile work despite having no experience at all

-expecting a friend who is a plumber/electrician/carpenter to do the work for free

-skipping the home inspection because all the work just looked like cosmetic stuff

Here are the stories about a few successful flippers I have worked with.

Mr. Fu invested in real estate in California for about 10 years. He decided to relocate to Texas during the severe market dive in California. He really loved his work, and he didn't want to stop doing it just because property values were falling on the west coast.

Since the market remained relatively stable in Texas, he decided to try the same techniques he used in San Diego in Austin. He knew he would be starting over with new contractors and REO brokers, but Mr. Fu had a secret weapon. His secret weapon was Mrs. Fu.

Mrs. Fu owned her own home-staging company in San Diego and happily opened her second staging showroom in Austin. Every home Mr. Fu flipped received the special attention of Mrs. Fu before it went on the market. She chose furnishings that truly fit each room to maximize the perception of space. If a bedroom was small, she chose a twin bed and a small arm chair. Simple wall decorations, mirrors in low-light hallways, and area rugs were all the elements of her domain. She chose crown molding, chair rails, bead board, and other features uncommonly found in entry level homes to up the "wow" factor of each property. Mrs. Fu also designed the landscaping.

As a result of their joint efforts, Mr. and Mrs. Fu always got top dollar for their homes. Buyers gasped when they entered every doorway. Sometimes buyers gasped when they pulled up to the curb. They knew they were successful when other investors and builders started calling Mrs. Fu and asking for quotes for her services.

Chapter 13

First Home Purchase

If you don't yet own a home yourself and you really want to get started as a rental real estate investor there is a way for you to do both simultaneously. If you don't have a lot of money but you do have a reliable source of income, check to see if an FHA home loan is right for you. At this time the down payment required is 3.5% of the purchase price of the home. If you buy a $300,000 home, this means you need $10,500 to put down as your initial investment. What many people don't know, however, is that you can get an FHA loan for a property that is up to 4 units. Yes! You could buy your first home and have 3 rentals right away.

If you like the idea but want to start a little smaller, see if you can find a duplex in your area. You could live in one side and rent the other one.

Chapter 14

A Brief Word on Unusual Rental Strategies

The real estate market in Detroit is probably one of the saddest stories of our generation. At this time it is one of those rare places where you can buy a standing home for less than you can spend to build one. However, two years ago I sold two properties there to an industrious elderly woman who made lemonade out of lemons. After a series of financial pitfalls she started renting out the rooms in her house. Pretty soon she had plenty of money to fund her monthly living expenses again. When she realized she could buy two houses on her street for $5,000 each, she picked up two and rented out the rooms in them as well. She called them her Rooming Houses. She went from being very concerned about her retirement years to making over $50,000 a year in Detroit rental income. Not many seasoned investors can say that. She was local and knew her market, she was close enough to manage the properties herself, and she started out small. She is still the investor I worked with whom I admire the most.

Chapter 15

Wrapping Up

You know enough now to formulate your own rental strategy. Don't forget to write it all out before you start shopping! Make an Excel spreadsheet, write an e-mail to yourself, write it on a Steno pad, whatever you need to do to make it work for *you*. Study your market, watch your budget, borrow sensibly, and find your own secret weapons. Good luck getting rich with your rentals!

Valuable Websites

www.craigslist.org

List your rentals and homes for sale on craigslist. Look for distressed homes offered for sale here, too.

www.GoSection8.com

To list your properties available for Section 8 tenants. This is also a good source to see what bedroom counts in your area rent for each month.

www.hudhomestore.com

To shop low priced inventories of houses by state.

www.Trulia.com

To search listed homes for sale or rent in a certain area. Also to check neighboring property values.

www.google.com/alert

Here you can set up a daily or weekly alert. I set up alerts for [City Name Here Real Estate] via this site. Every day I get one e-mail with everything new that hit the internet that day. I see YouTube videos, newspaper articles, and specific addresses that relate to real estate for the city I watch in one simple e-mail.

www.zillow.com

To check neighboring property values. Please note: "Zestimates" can be very general and should not be the only number you use to determine what a property is worth. I have seen these estimates in error by more than $500,000.

www.docusign.com

This is the easiest way to send contract paperwork back and forth for signatures. This has saved me days if not weeks-worth of time. Forget the fax machine, mail, or courier. This is simply the best way to go until you need a notary public to witness your signature.